Practice Papers

English

AGE 9–11

Robin Brown
Chartered Educational Psychologist

This book has been devised to improve your child's performance in selection examinations. It gives you the opportunity to work together towards success in gaining a place at the school of your choice.

Advice on what you can do to help your child is given overleaf. At the centre of the book (pages 15–18) you will find a pull-out section containing answers for each paper and a 'Test Profile' to chart your child's progress, together with questions to help your child learn from any mistakes.

ISBN 0 340 72687 3

Text © Robin Brown 1998

The right of Robin Brown to be identified as the author of this work has been asserted by him in accordance with the Copyright, Design and Patents Act 1988.

First published as a W. H. Smith exclusive 1995, this edition published 1998.

All rights reserved. No part of this book may be reproduced, stored in a retrieval system, or transmitted, in any form or by any means, without the prior written permission of the publisher, nor be otherwise circulated in any form of binding or cover other than that in which it is published and without a similar condition being imposed on the subsequent purchaser.

Published by Hodder Children's Books, a division of Hodder Headline plc, 338 Euston Road, London NW1 3BH

Printed and bound in Great Britain

A CIP record is registered by and held at the British Library

The only home learning programme supported by the NCPTA

TIPS FOR PARENTS

- The practice papers within this book offer your child the opportunity to experience questions similar to those that appear in assessment tests around the country. The tests have been designed to give your child an understanding of the principles involved and to increase self-confidence.

- 'Helpful Hints' are provided at the end of each practice paper. These offer guidance in answering particular types of questions and also recommend valuable study techniques. Encourage your child to cover over this section and only to look at it once the paper has been completed.

- Encourage the development of good exam practice such as:
  - looking over the paper quickly before starting
  - reading the questions carefully and answering exactly what is asked for
  - answering first the questions that you can answer and then the questions that you find difficult
  - planning your time carefully and working at a steady pace
  - staying calm and doing your best

- Allow 45 minutes for each practice paper.

- Do not allow the use of a dictionary when answering any of the questions, but encourage your child to look up any unfamiliar words afterwards.

- Go through the completed paper with your child and read the 'Helpful Hints' that follow. Discuss the 'Test Profile' questions on page 18 and enter their test score on the graph.

- Encourage your child to explain the reasons for giving a particular answer. By explaining the route to an answer, your child's understanding of that type of question will be strengthened and any mistakes will be learnt from. In practice papers such as these, learning how to improve performance is as important as the results in the preparation for future tests.

- Remember to make the tests enjoyable, to praise successes and to build up your child's confidence.

- Analyse the type of questions your child finds difficult and try to give more practice on these.

PRACTICE PAPER 1

Read the following passage carefully and then answer the questions below:

April 1st is commonly referred to as April Fool's Day and is a day which is renowned for practical jokes. In one famous hoax on television the presenter, Richard Dimbleby, solemnly announced to the viewers of 'Panorama' on 1st April 1957 that a record spaghetti harvest had just taken place in southern Switzerland. There then followed pictures of trees laden with strands of spaghetti, accompanied by interviews with local farmers rejoicing at the largest spaghetti harvest for 20 years.

Hundreds of viewers rang the BBC wanting to know where they could buy spaghetti plants. Producer Michael Peacock informed them that many British enthusiasts got admirable results from planting a small tin of spaghetti in tomato sauce. When the same viewers read in the paper on the following day that the report of the bumper spaghetti harvest was a hoax they could not believe how gullible they had been. The spaghetti in the pictures had just been draped over the trees and the 'farmers' were actors.

(Adapted from *The Guinness Book of Amazing Records*)

1 What is April 1st known as? _____

2 In which country was the spaghetti meant to have grown? _____

3 In what year was the programme first screened? _____

4 Who was the producer of the programme? _____

5 What was the name of the programme? _____

PRACTICE PAPER 1

6 Put these sentences in the correct order by writing the numbers 1 to 5 in the boxes. The first sentence should be shown by the number 1 and the last sentence by number 5:

a ☐ The viewers ring to find out where to buy spaghetti plants.

b ☐ A producer thinks of an idea for the programme.

c ☐ The newspapers report that the programme was a hoax.

d ☐ The programme is screened on television.

e ☐ The BBC film spaghetti on the trees and interview the actors who are pretending to be farmers.

7 Did these events happen in the last 10 years? _____

8 Write TRUE or FALSE after each of these sentences:

a The programme was shown on radio. _____

b Richard Dimbleby was the presenter. _____

c BBC stands for British Broadcasting Circus. _____

d The spaghetti harvest was supposed to have taken place in northern Switzerland. _____

e The newspapers described the programme as a hoax the day before it was screened. _____

9 Underline the most appropriate answer to each question:

a People rang the BBC because they were

    1 bored   2 angry   3 interested   4 hungry

b Spaghetti does not grow from tins because it is

    1 grown on trees   2 produced in factories
    3 grown underground   4 caught in nets

c The farmers in the programme described the spaghetti harvest because they were

    1 farmers   2 actors   3 criminals   4 producers

PRACTICE PAPER 1

    d The BBC produced this programme because they
        1 like to lie   2 thought it was true
        3 report farming news   4 have a sense of humour

10 Here are some words from the passage. On the right is a list of their meanings. Match each word with its meaning and write the correct number in the brackets:

a	hoax	( )	1	crop
b	famous	( )	2	duped, easily taken in
c	harvest	( )	3	substance shaped like a string
d	strand	( )	4	person who is full of zeal
e	gullible	( )	5	well-known
f	enthusiast	( )	6	deception by way of a joke

11 Underline the word which has the opposite meaning to the word in capitals:

a	ROUGH	round	humble	smooth	large
b	TOP	below	bottom	above	lower
c	EXPENSIVE	expansive	poor	cheap	small
d	INNOCENT	famous	beautiful	superior	guilty
e	PROSPERITY	poverty	mean	thrifty	generous

12 Give the plurals of the following:

a bag _____ b dress _____

c sheep _____ d bus _____

e ox _____ f box _____

g mouse _____ h scarf _____

i goose _____

PRACTICE PAPER 1

13 Homonyms are words that sound the same but have different spellings and meanings. Underline the correct word in the brackets.
Allow one mark for each correct word.

   a   Mustapha bought the shirt in a (sail, sale).

   b   The ship docked at the (quay, key).

   c   The (boy, buoy) ate his delicious (dessert, desert).

   d   (Their, There) was an eerie sound coming from the (cellar, seller) under the house.

   e   The boat was carried along by a strong (currant, current) as the (tied, tide) went out.

   f   The (deer, dear) escaped through the (whole, hole) in the fence.

HELPFUL HINTS

1–5   These questions are designed to test your ability to extract facts from the story. Read the questions *carefully* and make sure that your answers are exactly what is asked for. For example, in **4**, you are asked to name the *producer* of the programme. Two names are mentioned in the passage, the presenter and the producer, so be careful to name the correct one.

6   This is testing your ability to analyse information, compare it to the story and sequence it in the correct order. For example, the programme cannot be screened *before* the producer has thought of the idea for it.

7–9   You have to use information given in the story and, in some cases, common sense to make a judgement. For example, for **7**, you are told the programme was shown in 1957 so the events could not have happened in the last 10 years. In **8a**, programmes cannot be shown on a radio, only heard, so the answer is 'false'. In **9d**, the programme was a hoax for April Fool's Day, which suggests the programme's producers have a sense of humour.

10–13   At the end of the test, use a dictionary to check any words you are unsure of.

PRACTICE PAPER 2

Read the passage below carefully and then answer the questions that follow:

A Swiss cheese fondue is traditionally heated at the table in a communal pot called a 'caquelon'. Cheese is melted in the pot with wine and is kept warm by a spirit burner underneath. When the fondue is ready to eat and everyone is sitting around the table, each person spears a cube of bread on a fondue fork and swirls it in the fondue until coated in cheese. This delicious morsel of coated bread is then eaten and savoured.

This traditional Swiss dish is now a popular meal for parties with friends. However, fondues were originally developed because of the climate and terrain in Switzerland. In winter, when many mountain villages were cut off by heavy snow falls, fresh food was scarce and each village was forced to rely on its own resources. The locally produced foods such as bread, wine and cheese were their main diet. As winter dragged on, the cheese became dry and hard. However, it was discovered that melting this dry, hard cheese with wine made a delicious meal and so the Swiss cheese fondue was born. Although the idea remains the same, the different cantons of Switzerland are famous for their variations of this basic recipe.

The traditional 'caquelon' was an earthenware pot, but cast-iron fondue pots will serve just as well. Copper or stainless steel pots are sometimes used but these tend to be made of thin metal and the cheese can easily burn in them.

(Adapted from *Fondue Cookery* by Alison Burt)

PRACTICE PAPER 2

1 In which country were fondues first developed? _____

2 What is a traditional fondue pot called? _____

3 Is a fondue a cold or a warm meal? _____

4 What liquid is used with cheese in a fondue? _____

5 Why were the villages cut off in winter?

_____

6 What happened to the cheese over the winter?

_____

7 What is the problem if the metal fondue pot is too thin?

_____

8 Use the information in the passage to help you underline the most appropriate answer:

   a The fondue pot is kept warm by
      1 electricity   2 gas   3 spirit burner   4 coal fire

   b Switzerland has a lot of
      1 fish   2 mountains   3 forests   4 rivers   5 cooks

   c What is dipped into a fondue?
      1 your finger   2 spears   3 wine   4 bread on a fork

   d A canton is a
      1 district or region   2 mountain   3 cooking pot
      4 type of bread   5 person

   e Traditional fondue pots are
      1 copper   2 zinc   3 wooden   4 earthenware   5 thin

9 Write TRUE or FALSE after each of these statements.

   a Fondues were only invented for parties. _____

PRACTICE PAPER 2

    b   There is only one recipe for making a fondue.   _____

    c   Cheese is used in making a fondue.   _____

    d   Fondue pots cannot be made out of cast iron.   _____

10   Here are some words from the passage. On the right is a list of their meanings. Match each word with its meaning and write the correct number in the brackets:

a	communal	( )	1	well-liked
b	swirls	( )	2	well-known
c	delicious	( )	3	shared by a group
d	morsel	( )	4	a different version
e	climate	( )	5	stirs about
f	terrain	( )	6	rare, hard to find
g	famous	( )	7	tasty
h	popular	( )	8	tiny piece or mouthful
i	scarce	( )	9	the geography of an area
j	variation	( )	10	typical weather for a region

11   Complete each sentence by adding an occupation from the list below:

    florist   plumber   dentist   pilot

    cobbler   referee   optician   journalist

    a   A _____ mends burst pipes and blocked drains.

    b   The _____ made sure the footballers kept to the rules.

    c   I bought a bunch of flowers from the _____ .

    d   I had my eyesight tested by the _____ .

    e   The _____ repaired my shoes.

PRACTICE PAPER 2

    f   The _____ brought the plane in to land.

    g   The _____ writes articles for the local newspaper.

    h   I had my teeth checked by the _____ .

12 FONDUE begins with FO. Complete these words which also begin with FO:

    a   At the end of your leg.   FO _____

    b   A silly person.   FO _____

    c   The base on which the building rests.   FO _____

    d   Two weeks.   FO _____

    e   Group of trees.   FO _____

    f   Not remember.   FO _____

13 Form nouns from the words on the left to complete each sentence:

    a   DESCRIBE   The _____ of the suspect was accurate.

    b   INVITE   She gave out the _____ to the party.

    c   SERVE   The _____ in the restaurant was very slow.

    d   EXPLODE   The _____ was very loud.

    e   LAUGH   The _____ filled the theatre.

    f   INJURE   The footballer's _____ was not serious.

    g   ARRIVE   The next _____ is due any minute.

    h   PUNISH   It was an unpleasant _____ .

    i   ADVERTISE   The _____ was very successful.

    j   COLLECT   A _____ was taken up for the charity.

PRACTICE PAPER 2

HELPFUL HINTS

1 Make sure you write the name of the country – Switzerland – and not *Swiss* which describes the people or traditions of Switzerland.

8e Although you are told that fondue pots can be made out of copper, the passage states that the traditional *caquelons*, or pots, were earthenware.

9b The answer is 'false' because you are told that there are *variations* of the basic recipe.

9d Although you are told that the traditional *caquelons* were earthenware pots, you are also told that a cast-iron fondue pot will serve just as well. So the answer is 'false' because cast-iron *can* be used.

PRACTICE PAPER 3

Read the passage below carefully and then underline or write in the correct answers to the questions that follow:

'This must be a simply enormous wardrobe!' thought Lucy, going still further in and pushing the soft folds of the coats aside to make room for her. Then she noticed that there was something crunching under her feet. 'I wonder is that mothballs?' she thought, stooping down to feel it with her hand. But instead of feeling the hard, smooth wood of the floor of the wardrobe, she felt something soft and powdery and extremely cold. 'This is very queer,' she said, and went on a step or two further.

Next moment she found that what was rubbing against her face and hands was no longer soft fur but something hard and rough and even prickly. 'Why, it is just like branches of trees!' exclaimed Lucy. And then she saw that there was a light ahead of her; not a few inches away where the back of the wardrobe ought to have been, but a long way off. Something cold and soft was falling on her. A moment later she found that she was standing in the middle of a wood at night-time with snow under her feet and snowflakes falling through the air.

Lucy felt a little frightened, but she felt very inquisitive and excited as well. She looked back over her shoulder and there, between the dark tree trunks, she could still see the open doorway of the wardrobe and even catch a glimpse of the empty room from which she had set out.

(From *The Lion, the Witch and the Wardrobe* by C. S. Lewis)

1 What do you think Lucy had stepped into at the beginning of this story?
    a the road   **b** a wardrobe   **c** a puddle   **d** her bed

2 What did Lucy have to move aside?
    a a dog   **b** a door   **c** her sister   **d** the coats

PRACTICE PAPER 3

3 What crunched under Lucy's feet?

    a glass   **b** snow   **c** mothballs   **d** a wooden floorboard

4 How would you describe the thing that rubbed against Lucy's face?

    a hard and smooth   **b** hard and rough
    c soft and cold   **d** soft and powdery

5 What fell on Lucy?

    a a tree   **b** a coat   **c** an animal   **d** snowflakes

6 How did Lucy feel?

    a frightened   **b** tired   **c** happy   **d** sad

7 What does *inquisitive* mean?

    a innocent   **b** frightened   **c** excited   **d** curious

8 When do you think this story took place?

    a 1856   **b** dawn   **c** night-time   **d** day-time

9 Where did Lucy end up?

    a in a wardrobe   **b** in an empty room   **c** in a wood   **d** in bed

10 Where had Lucy come from?

    a an empty room   **b** another planet   **c** London   **d** a wood

11 Would you find the book that this passage is taken from in the fiction or non-fiction section of the library? _____

PRACTICE PAPER 3

12 Complete the following sentences with 'there', 'their' or 'they're':

   a He left his bag over _____ .

   b The teacher gave them _____ books.

   c _____ going to miss the bus if they stay any longer.

   d If _____ here we can start the lesson.

   e Is _____ a doctor to help the child?

   f He left _____ tickets for the concert at home.

13 Write the exact words which were spoken in these sentences:

   a 'Have you eaten your tea?' asked his father.

   _____

   b 'Look out!' shouted Jane. _____

   c Peter told Mike to sit up. _____

   d 'Come inside,' said the teacher, 'and take off your coats.'

   _____

   e The policeman shouted to the boys to stop.

   _____

14 Underline the word which has the opposite meaning to the word in capitals:

a	FIRST	ninth	last	second	fourth	third
b	LITTLE	small	full	empty	wide	big
c	ROUGH	square	round	smooth	rigid	
d	DEFEAT	define	victory	valour	brave	afraid
e	INSIDE	internal	warmer	colder	interior	outside
f	BEST	winner	last	worst	better	bigger
g	SAFE	deceived	dangerous	delayed	definite	

PRACTICE PAPER 3

15 Underline the word in the brackets which completes the pattern:

    a   Sky is to blue as coal is to (white, black, yellow).

    b   Carrot is to vegetable as apple is to (pie, drink, fruit, orange).

    c   Fish is to sea as bird is to (house, cat, wing, sky).

    d   Wheel is to car as wing is to (plane, ship, bicycle, house).

Now underline one word from each bracket to complete the pattern.
Allow 1 mark for each correct word.

    e   Snow is to white as (stone, hair, grass) is to (green, food, cricket).

    f   Rabbit is to hutch as (house, horse, cat) is to (air, dog, stable).

    g   Mother is to father as (cousin, teacher, sister) is to (tractor, brother, uncle).

    h   Dog is to bark as (lion, wolf, lamb) is to (bleat, snore, shout).

16 Underline the two words that must change places for the sentences to make sense, e.g. The attendant put the <u>car</u> in the <u>petrol</u>.
There is one mark for each pair of words correctly underlined.

    a   The potatoes harvested a large crop of farmer.

    b   The mechanic changed the tyre flat.

    c   The famous chef banquet the prepared for the special guests.

    d   The climber stood on the summit and before at the breathtaking views over the mountain range looked him.

    e   The ambulance warn the siren to sounded the other motorists that they were on an emergency call.

PRACTICE PAPER 3

17 Read this description of a holiday cottage and then answer FACT or OPINION to best describe the statements below:

'Hideaway' is a stone-built cottage 3 miles from the famous beach at Lipton. Imaginatively converted, this cottage has retained the original fireplaces and oak beams. The owners describe the cottage as the perfect place to get away from it all in the most scenic countryside in Britain. Set in 2 acres of garden, the cottage overlooks the cliffs and offers numerous gentle walks to coves and villages along the coast.

a   The cottage is called 'Hideaway'. _____

b   There is a beach at Lipton. _____

c   The cottage has been 'imaginatively' converted. _____

d   The cottage has 2 acres of garden. _____

e   It is a gentle walk from the cottage to the coves. _____

f   The cottage is the perfect place to get away from it all. _____

g   The cottage has a fireplace. _____

h   The cottage is 3 miles from a beach. _____

HELPFUL HINTS

4 Make sure that your answers are exactly what is asked for. For example, in **4**, you are asked for the description of what *rubbed against Lucy's face*. Although snow, which was decribed as 'cold and soft', fell on her, you are told that what was rubbing against her face was something hard and rough, so the correct answer is **b**.

12 Remember that 'they're' is short for 'they are', as in **c**.

17 A fact is something that is true or can be measured, while an opinion expresses a person's viewpoint, which may differ from the views of others. So it is a fact that the cottage is called 'Hideaway' but to describe it as 'imaginatively' converted is a matter of opinion.

PRACTICE PAPER 4

Read this passage to find out what the different people think about holidays and use this information to help you answer the questions that follow:

Mr Smith: 'We always pick holidays that are near the beach with lots of activities for the children.'

Mr Patel: 'I do not like flying so I always take the car on the ferry across the Channel and go camping in France.'

Mrs Arnold: 'I hate cooking but love any kind of sport so I tend to choose hotels that have good leisure facilities.'

Miss Soames: 'I think spending all that money on two weeks abroad is a waste, especially when the money could be used to help people in need.'

Mr Ford: 'My wife and I could never just sit on a beach. We love passing the time shopping and looking around art galleries and museums.'

Read each statement below and then decide which person was most likely to have said it:

1 'Every day I went swimming or played tennis before having lunch in the hotel.' _____

2 'The children enjoyed making sandcastles by the sea.' _____

PRACTICE PAPER 4

3 'We spent far too much but the paintings and clothes were so much cheaper than back at home.' _____

4 'I gave the money I would have spent on a holiday to charity and then enjoyed a week at home.' _____

5 'My husband enjoyed the Natural History Museum but my favourite was the Tate Gallery.' _____

6 'It was a terrible gale and the crossing was very rough.' _____

7 'The children enjoyed the holiday because there was so much for them to do.' _____

8 'You can't beat sleeping under canvas in a foreign country.' _____

9 'The cuisine in the hotel was excellent.' _____

10 Rearrange the following words in alphabetical order:

   a   satchel   sandwich   scaffold   scald   sack

   _____

   b   exuberant   extravagant   extreme   edge   exception

   _____

   c   dialect   diagnosis   distort   delegate   diary

   _____

   d   modify   mitten   moment   mouth   monkey   mouse

   _____

   e   voice   verdict   volume   vessel   view   verb

   _____

   f   ready   register   reason   refresh   read   refuge

   _____

PRACTICE PAPER 4

11 Underline the word in the right-hand column which goes with the words in the left-hand column:

a	London	Cardiff	Glasgow	England	France	Leeds	
b	cod	plaice	haddock	horse	salmon	donkey	boy
c	kitten	calf	cygnet	puppy	cow	whale	duck
d	car	bus	bicycle	boat	helicopter	bed	coach
e	oboe	clarinet	cello	flute	pencil	brush	net
f	rectangle	square	circle	octagon	octopus	planet	ball
g	purple	green	pink	grass	brown	leaves	tree

12 Underline the word which describes the home of each animal:

a	HORSE	house	burrow	tree	stable	den
b	BIRD	stable	sea	nest	hive	hospital
c	DOG	church	kennel	book	net	pool
d	BEE	nest	hive	cage	pond	tree
e	PIG	box	stable	shell	nest	sty
f	WASP	net	hive	nest	lodge	lair

13 Underline one word in each pair of brackets so that the passage makes sense. *Allow 1 mark for each correct answer.*

The pupils put away their (ears, books, lions), collected (there, their) bags and then lined up to wait for the (tanker, rocket, bus). Thursday was swimming (day, month, year) for the pupils of class 6 and there was great excitement as they (travelled, slept, wrote) to the pool. Angela was looking forward to trying the test to (jump, swim, hop) one length of breast-stroke to win another badge to sew on her swimming (car, leg, costume).

PRACTICE PAPER 4

14 Underline the two words in each line which rhyme with each other.
There is one mark for each correct pair of rhyming words.

    a   poor   pair   foot   five   fair   port

    b   hair   mouse   mark   house   march   fort

    c   place   palace   plank   plaice   peach

    d   hole   walk   heart   whale   whole   week

    e   peel   late   meat   lark   meal   mute

    f   bought   beach   bike   beauty   beech   beaver

15 Rewrite the following words with the prefix un–, in–, dis– or im–
to make a new word with the opposite meaning:

    a   employed   _____

    b   appear   _____

    c   allow   _____

    d   likely   _____

    e   possible   _____

    f   complete   _____

    g   dependent   _____

    h   happy   _____

    i   obey   _____

HELPFUL HINTS

1–9 You have to use the information you are given to make certain deductions. For example, in **5**, the statement tells you that the person enjoys galleries or museums so this would match with what you are told about Mr and Mrs Ford. As the statement refers to 'My husband', it must be <u>Mrs</u> Ford who is making the statement.

13 If you cannot choose a word, read on and come back to it. Information you are given later in the passage may help you to decide which word to choose.

PRACTICE PAPER 5

Read the passage below and then answer the questions that follow:

'They're not for sale,' Mr Wonka answered. 'She can't have one.'

'Who says I can't!' shouted Veruca. 'I'm going in to get myself one this very minute!'

'Don't!' said Mr Wonka quickly, but he was too late. The girl had already thrown open the door and rushed in.

The moment she entered the room, one hundred squirrels stopped what they were doing and turned their heads and stared at her with small black beady eyes.

Veruca Salt stopped also, and stared back at them. Then her gaze fell upon a pretty little squirrel sitting nearest to her at the end of the table. The squirrel was holding a walnut in its paws.

'All right,' Veruca said, 'I'll have you!'

She reached out her hands to grab the squirrel … but as she did so … in that first split second when her hands started to go forward, there was a sudden flash of movement in the room, like a flash of brown lightning, and every single squirrel around the table took a flying leap towards her and landed on her body.

Twenty-five of them caught hold of her right arm, and pinned that down. Twenty-five more caught hold of her left arm, and pinned that down. Twenty-five caught hold of her right leg and anchored it to the ground. Twenty-four caught hold of her left leg. And the one remaining squirrel (obviously the leader of them all) climbed up on to her shoulder and started tap-tap-tapping the wretched girl's head with its knuckles.

'Save her!' screamed Mrs Salt. 'Veruca! Come back! What are they doing to her?'

'They're testing her to see if she's a bad nut,' said Mr Wonka. 'You watch.'

(From *Charlie and the Chocolate Factory* by Roald Dahl)

PRACTICE PAPER 5

1 What did Veruca want to buy? _____

2 How many squirrels were in the room? _____

3 What is Veruca's surname? _____

4 What was the squirrel at the end of the table holding? _____

5 Who is the author of this book? _____

6 Underline the most appropriate answer to each question:

    a Veruca could be best described as

        1 polite and genteel   2 obnoxious and rude

        3 strong and kind   4 observant

    b The squirrels held Veruca by the

        1 left arm alone   2 hand

        3 the arms and legs   4 shoulder

    c The leader of the squirrels tapped Veruca's head with

        1 a hammer   2 an anchor

        3 a pin   4 his knuckles

    d Mrs Salt's reaction to these events can be described as

        1 happy   2 anxious   3 content   4 calm

7 Write TRUE or FALSE after each of these statements:

    a Mr Wonka was selling squirrels. _____

    b The squirrels had black eyes. _____

    c Veruca stroked the squirrels gently. _____

    d The squirrels moved very quickly. _____

    e Mr Wonka pulled the squirrels off Veruca. _____

PRACTICE PAPER 5

8 Put these sentences in the same order as in the story by writing the numbers 1 to 5 in the boxes. The first sentence in the story should be shown by the number 1 and the last sentence by 5:

a ☐ The leader of the squirrels tapped Veruca on the head.

b ☐ Veruca went to grab a squirrel.

c ☐ The squirrels stopped and stared at Veruca.

d ☐ The squirrels jumped at Veruca and held her down.

e ☐ Veruca entered the room.

9 Here are some words from the passage. On the right is a list of their meanings. Match each word with its meaning and write the number in the brackets:

a	pretty ( )	1	secured
b	screamed ( )	2	looked closely
c	stared ( )	3	attractive
d	beady ( )	4	uttered a piercing cry
e	anchored ( )	5	displeasing, contemptible
f	leap ( )	6	small and bright
g	wretched ( )	7	jump

10 Write a suitable collective noun or group name in each space:

a   a _____ athletes   b   a _____ of wolves

c   a _____ of drawers   d   a _____ of bees

e   a _____ of sheep   f   a _____ of grapes

11 Give the meanings of the abbreviations in italics:

a   It was 120 *cm* long.   _____

PRACTICE PAPER 5

b Mrs Jones was the elected *MP* for the area.

_____

c He ran for the team representing the *UK*. _____

d The Liverpool *v* Celtic game was a draw. _____

12 Complete each sentence with an adverb formed from the word in capitals:

   a GRACEFUL   The ballerina danced _____.

   b CARE   He copied the work _____.

   c SILENCE   He crept up on him _____.

   d ACCIDENT   She _____ broke the plate.

   e COMFORT   Jane was lying _____ on the couch.

13 The following words end in –ent or –ant. Add the correct ending to each one:

   a governm_____   **b** par_____

   c indign_____   **d** independ_____

   e gr_____   **f** appointm_____

14 Put the word in capitals into the past tense to complete each sentence:

   a CATCH   She _____ the ball and John was out.

   b DESCRIBE   The man _____ the missing car.

   c RIDE   She _____ on the horse to the village.

HELPFUL HINTS

6–8 You have to use the information given in the story to make deductions or judgements. For example, in **6b**, although Veruca was held by the left arm, she was not *only* held by this but also by her right arm *and* legs. Therefore the correct answer is **3** and not **1**.

7d You are told that the squirrels moved like a 'flash of lightning', so it is 'true' that they moved very quickly.

PRACTICE PAPER 6

Read the information in the passage and the boxes to answer the questions that follow:

ASIA

Asia is the world's biggest continent, stretching from the cold Arctic Ocean in the north, to the warm Indian Ocean in the tropical south. Mainland Asia nearly reaches the equator in Malaysia. Several Asian islands are on the Equator: Sumatra, Borneo and Sulawesi. In the west, Asia reaches Europe and the Mediterranean Sea, and in the east Asia reaches the Pacific Ocean, and gets closer to Australia. In the centre are the high, empty plateaux of Tibet and Mongolia. The world's ten highest mountains are all in the Himalayas.

Over half the world's population lives in Asia. The coastal areas of South and East Asia are the most crowded parts. Six of the 'top ten' most populated countries in the world are in Asia: China, India, Indonesia, Japan, Bangladesh and Pakistan.

FACT BOX: ASIA

AREA: 44,387,000 sq km.

HIGHEST POINT: Mount Everest, 8,848 metres (Nepal/China).

LOWEST POINT: Shores of the Dead Sea, 400 metres below sea-level (Israel/Jordan).

LONGEST RIVER: Yenisei, 5,540 km.

SMALLEST COUNTRY: Maldives, 298 sq km.

MONEY IN SOME ASIAN COUNTRIES

Burma:	kyat
China:	yuan
Israel:	shekel
Japan:	yen
Maldives:	rufiya
Thailand:	baht
Turkey:	lira

(Adapted from *Philip's Children's Atlas* by David and Jill Wright)

1 Name the longest river in Asia. _____

2 Name an Asian island that is on the Equator. _____

3 Which is the smallest country in Asia? _____

PRACTICE PAPER 6

4 What is *sq km* an abbreviation of? _____

5 Which ocean is to the north of Asia? _____

6 Which ocean is to the east of Asia? _____

7 Which continent is to the west of Asia? _____

8 What is the currency in Thailand? _____

9 Underline the most appropriate answer to each question:

   a The Indian Ocean could be described as being in a region which is
      1 topical   2 cold   3 arctic   4 tropical

   b The highest point in Asia is
      1 Japan   2 Mount Yenisei   3 Mount Everest   4 Jordan

   c 'Population' refers to the number of
      1 mountains   2 inhabitants   3 currency   4 influences

   d The passage tells you that the plateaux of Tibet are
      1 high and wet   2 high and well populated
      3 empty and high   4 wet and empty

10 Write TRUE or FALSE after each of these sentences:

   a The Arctic Ocean is cold. _____

   b Six of the world's highest mountains are in the Himalayas. _____

   c The currency of Japan is the yuan. _____

   d India is one of the top ten most populated countries in the world. _____

   e The lowest point in Asia is in China. _____

11 Underline the word which has the same or a similar meaning to the first word in capitals:

   a POOR   rich   wealthy   poverty   difficult

   b ROUND   flat   circular   square   triangular

PRACTICE PAPER 6

    c   EMPTY   hollow   full   complete   smooth

    d   TIDY   clothes   neat   shabby   flat   thaw

    e   OLD   new   young   article   anvil   aged

    f   SQUEEZE   catch   squash   laugh   run   drop

    g   RAMBLE   chase   run   jump   stroll   swim

    h   STEAL   give   charity   thieve   honour   thump

12 Look at the clues and fill in the missing letters:

    a   _ o u _ l e   A pair.

    b   _ o _ s e   An animal you can ride.

    c   h o _ _ i t a _   A building where medical staff work.

    d   n _ g l _ c t   Leave uncared for.

    e   _ e a _ o c _   Bird with bright plumage.

    f   _ e c _ a n _ l e   Shape with four sides.

13 The jumbled words below are all about measurement. Rearrange the letters and write the correct words in the brackets. *Allow 1 mark for each correct answer.*

There are one hundred enticmtrees (   ) in a treme (   ). I use a ruler to measure my geihth (   ).
I use a optstchaw (   ) to time myself to see how fast I can run. There are sixty donssec (   ) in neo (   ) minute and xiyts (   ) minutes in one ruoh (   ). There are a thousand samgr (   ) in a kilogramme. I stand on the scales to ghwei (   ) myself.

14 Write these sentences with the correct punctuation:

    a   the man bought apples pears grapes and oranges

         _____

    b   have you seen my coat asked jenny

         _____

PRACTICE PAPER 6

   c   i must run said paul or i will miss my train
   _____

   d   parminder asked what time will you meet me
   _____

15 Complete the following proverbs:
   a   A bird in the hand is worth two in the _____ .
   b   Don't put _____ your eggs in one basket.
   c   First come, first _____ .

16 Idioms are expressions which are used in everyday conversation.
   Underline the phrase which means the same as the expression in italics:
   a   *To be behind the times*
       1   to be early   2   to be late   3   to be old-fashioned   4   supportive
   b   *I'm all ears*
       1   to have big ears   2   to be listening attentively
       3   to ignore   4   to be clumsy

HELPFUL HINTS

1–10 The information given here is typical of that found in many reference books. Be careful to give the answer that is asked for. For example, in **7**, you are asked for the *continent* which is to the west of Asia so the answer is Europe and not the Mediterranean Sea which appears in the same sentence and is also to the west of Asia.

The exercises test your ability to refer back to a text for facts or to use these facts to make judgements or deductions. For example, in **8**, 'currency' means the money used in a country so you need to look up 'Thailand' in the appropriate table. Also, in **10b** the answer is 'true' because you are told that the world's *ten* highest mountains are in the Himalayas so you can infer that *six* of the world's highest mountains must also be in the Himalayas.